25 KE

Po

OCPD's Only Hope of
Psychological Wellness!

Mack W. Ethridge

– The OCPD Person *MUST*

Ask! – And Have Answered!

OCPD's Only Hope of
Psychological Wellness!

Mack W. Ethridge

By Mack W. Ethridge, NFHR, Inc.

Award-Winning Writer, Researcher
Educator, Public Speaker

Copyright © 2018

by Mack W. Ethridge

Published by **New Frontier Health Research, Inc.**

Cover design by Mack W. Ethridge

Library of Congress Cataloging-in-Publications, Data, Ethridge, Mack W.

25 Key Questions the OCPD Person Must Ask! – Pocket Version
Complete edition

1st Complete Softback Edition, Sept. 2018

Author Qualifications (Partial)

Mack W. Ethridge is a seasoned professional writer/researcher/educator, as well as a life-long psychology major, who has devoted thousands of hours to the study of the Obsessive-Compulsive Personality Disorder, and draws upon his *first-hand* observations of this disorder in action. He has pioneered methods and techniques of how the OCPD person may best obtain **Insight** into their disorder, and thereby, pave the road to their recovery, and their full enjoyment of Life.

Not a stranger to the medical field, Mack has edited such prestigious periodicals as *The Journal of Neurosurgery*, of world-wide circulation; as well as such notable publications as *The Comprehensive Survey of Doctorate Recipients*, of The National Academy of Sciences; and, as a career editor, has received multiple commendations and awards. Mack has authored 30 OCPD books.

Disclaimer

All instruction or recommendations in this book are not in any fashion to be construed as medical advice, either for physical, psychological, or mental ailments. This research paper is not intended to diagnose the existence of OCPD, nor to prescribe treatment. Nor is it meant to professionally analyze the mental health condition or emotional fitness of the OCPD person. Self-assessment tools and related tables for the OCPD person (in the source 'Only Hope' volume) are provided _only_ to give an overall, general assessment, *likely* to be reflective of their present capacity to interact with society as a whole. But, only a qualified mental health practitioner can say for sure. In short, this book is meant for informational purposes, only. Before putting into practice any of its ideas or concepts, you would be well-advised to consult a certified health professional conversant with these matters.

The
Twenty-Five
(25)
KEY Questions
the OCPD Person
<u>**MUST**</u> Ask,

and Their
Practical Answers

Let Us Begin!

When I feel the **overwhelming need** to ***control*** another person, what can I do to quelch (*suppress,* or *silence*) this feeling?

To quelch your overwhelming need to control another person requires that you _first_ become **conscious** of this abnormal need seeking to manifest itself through me. (And you become conscious by being 'mindful' of the nature of your thoughts throughout the day. Such as by asking yourself, 'What is the real *intent* of these thoughts before I speak them?') Once you become aware, you can pause and remind yourself that controlling another is _not_ worthy of you and only creates resentment and hard feelings. A key liberating thought, here, is:

> ‘Seeking control of another is a disservice to <u>me</u>’

Once you have reminded yourself of this truth, you can then exercise your will power and **resist** your impulse to control another. So, the formula is: pause, become conscious, remind yourself your voicing these thoughts are <u>*not*</u> worthy of you, and exercise will power to resist misusing and/or abusing another. The **key**, here, is to recognize engaging in such activities is well beneath you, and is a disservice to YOU. **YOU** are deserving of better *if* you are to progressively develop, continually mature, and successively ‘evolve’ into a person of greater self-control and mastery in your life, resulting in your greater happiness. And a corollary to the above maxim is, **'Seeking to control another is a misuse of _them_.'** Use whichever Truth wording empowers you most to alter your behavior for the good.

When I feel the **strong urge** to _**criticize**_ my spouse, or coworker, or friend, how can I refrain from doing so?

To refrain from criticizing your spouse, or coworker, or friend when you are overtaken by a strong urge to do so (as in the case of when you were complaining), you must first become **conscious** of this urge seeking to express itself through you by mindfully reflecting upon what the nature of your thoughts are. Next, you must remind yourself that to unduly criticize another is rarely productive and is _a waste of **your** precious time._ Once you have reminded yourself of this Truth, you can then exercise your freedom of choice and resist your impulse to criticize another. The **key**, here, is to acknowledge to yourself the more you criticize, *the more you develop and entrench the habit of criticizing*. It becomes second nature (if not already your first), and you find yourself engaging in this activity more and more without even thinking. Take note of how you **feel** when you are criticizing another, it is never pleasant. And your face reflects this un-pleasantness (as may your acid-filled stomach). So, a key liberating thought is:

> '**Criticizing is a waste of <u>my</u> precious time, and often *only* results in distress**'

Then, tell yourself that you will _not_ criticize anyone (and then only constructively, and if <u>absolutely</u> necessary, as a boss to her employee, or parent to child) unless it is a matter of time/task efficiency, or a financial, health, safety, or a security concern.

When I find myself ***complaining***, constantly, about world events, the weather, how a natural disaster is handled by authorities, government policies, school board decisions, or most anything else, how can I **stop** myself from continuing?

<hr>

No. 3

You can stop complaining about world events, or natural disasters, or government policies, and the like, by first pausing and becoming **fully cognizant** that you are doing so. Next, you must tell yourself that the act of complaining only serves to <u>sour</u> your disposition on people and the world, and cause you to feel *down*. And not-to-mention, your complaining also causes those around you to look upon you as a 'whiner', 'one who 'belly-aches', and a 'cry-baby'. Once you have reminded yourself of this Truth, you can choose to stop complaining right then and there, and begin to talk about more pleasant, encouraging, uplifting, hopeful things. A **key**, liberating thought, here, is:

> **'When I stop complaining,
> I am _no longer_ contributing
> to the negativity of the world'**

This is a powerful thought, once you grasp its full significance, as it identifies YOU as a prime factor in either making the world a more desirable place to live in, or not. (Of course, there is a proper time and place to complain, but such occurrences almost always pertain to *official* complaints to proper authorities for rectification of injustices or the remedying of unsatisfactory or unacceptable situations.) Complaining for its own sake is harmful.

What is the best antidote to my constant ***worrying*** and ***fretting***?

The best antidote to the constant worrying you are so prone to do is to one, become **aware** you are in a mental worrying 'mode', and then two, pause sufficiently long enough to remind yourself that *your worry is a traitor to your cause*, that of your overall well-being and welfare.

A **key**, liberating thought is:

> **'Worry is a *useless* pastime, offering no real benefits'**

(Or, perhaps 'Worry is an _un-productive_ pastime.') Due to old habit thought patterns, you will initially feel this is not true. 'Does not worry cause me to explore the problem,' you ask yourself, 'and search for a solution?' **No**, it really does not. Worry consumes your precious life energy mas-querading as a benefactor, causing you to _repeatedly_ imagine all of the bad things that are 'sure' to occur. Once you recognize this, you can **decide** to stop ruminating over your situation or challenge (as does a cow unceasingly chewing its 'cud', or regurgitated food), and instead make up your mind to take physical ACTION (_doing_ something) to either alleviate or remedy the situation. Sitting around and just 'thinking' about the problem is a sure recipe for mental and emotional turmoil! Ponder your options, **yes**, consider your alternatives, **Yes**, evaluate what recourse is available to you, **YES**. But, do <u>not</u> dwell on the 'pros and cons' too long. Set a *time limit* during which you can ponder the problem, then turn your attention to some other entirely different matter. If you wish, you can come back to your 'worry time' – later, and resume! This will help you break the bad habit, in time.

People tell me that I am so ***negative*** all the time, yet I honestly do not feel that I am. How can I become more *aware* of this tendency? And distinguish what is truly negative and what is *not?*

You can become more aware of your tendency to be negative much of the time, again, by **realizing** what your mental state is. Here, again, **pause**, and ask yourself *'How do I feel?'* Your body will tell you in no uncertain terms as you become more practiced and proficient in listening to it. Soon, you will **immediately know** when you are in a negative mood, and will *immediately* perceive that your words, tone of voice, and facial expression are negative, which is to say, anything _but_ positive or optimistic. At first, your being negative will probably not be as easy to detect (to be perceived by you) as many might think. That is because negativity can be expressed either in a very pronounced way (loudly, with angry gestures), or in a more subtle, often consciously _un_detected way (softly, with calmness). A key, liberating thought is:

> '**I choose _not_ to be negative, either obviously, nor in a _less_ obvious fashion**'

But, what is _**truly**_ negative, even if spoken softly and slowly, **always** tends to cause you and those around you to feel despondent and sad. If after you have had a conversation with another (where <u>you</u> did most of the talking), and you find yourself feeling tired, lethargic, blasé, or apathetic, or lacking in enthusiasm, during or afterwards, then you can be certain the content of your discussion (or spirit of your discourse) was **negative**!

How can I determine, being a '***neat freak***', when I am investing too much time for my own good in working on organization, placement of objects, symmetry of arrangement, etc.? This seems so difficult!

_____ **No. 6** _____

You **can** know when you am investing *too* *much* *time* for your own good in working on organization, object placement, symmetry, and the like, when 1) you begin to personally experience *increasing levels of stress (or distress)* in attempting to find that highly-elusive 'perfect' arrangement. Or, 2) you may register in your consciousness the disquieting feeling that *other* more pressing and important matters are being neglected and not receiving proper attention. And, 3) other concerned people may volunteer their observation that you are becoming preoccupied with order at the expense of your peace of mind or the completing other household or professional tasks. A heart-lightening thought is:

'I can be neat and orderly *without* measuring down to the smallest fraction of an inch'

Remember, perceiving that you are becoming **nervous** is a dead giveaway! Don't become so 'invested' in a given 'placement project' that you become obsessively

locked into completing it – as it may take you all day and all night to do it! Listen to your body. If it tells you it needs a break from any given project, learn to heed its cautionary admonitions. Body wisdom speaks Truth.

How can I best combat my 'inescapably' **compelling desire** to be **_ultra-perfect_** in everything I do?

You can best combat your _seemingly_ inescapable compelling desire to be ultra-perfect in everything you do by realizing (and then periodically _re_-realizing!) _just how much_ such behavior is **costing you** in terms of peace of mind, inner harmony, and your physical health. We might phrase **a rescuing question** thus: Do you want to experience peace of mind, live with inner harmony, and enjoy vibrant, vital health, _OR_ do you want to uselessly, and even 'punishingly', pursue your ideal of 'perfection', which is always just out of your reach or full attainment? For once you initially feel you have found that 'perfect' dress, or 'perfect' car, or you have completed that 'perfect' term paper or ran that 'perfect' race, in a very short time you view it as *still* less than 'perfect'! Because you can <u>always</u> *imagine* a different (and God forbid the thought!), even a **better** way to *do* something, or *achieve* something, or to *be* something! A **key**, life affirming thought, then, is:

'I will <u>*not*</u> wait until the pain of pursuing 'perfection' incapacitates me, I'll heed its warnings, and <u>stop</u>!'

Thereafter, you can pursue **Excellence**, which is a high level of craftsmanship or superior performance, and be justifiably satisfied, but _not_ foolishly race after entrapping, life-mocking 'Perfection'! As that is, thankfully, God's province, <u>alone</u>!

Who am I to **deviate** from *any* **rule**, whether it be a state law, workplace policy, school or public park rule, or any other regulation? Shouldn't I be strictly observant of them as a good citizen, a loyal employee, or a supportive neighbor?

No. 8

Yes, you *should* be strictly observant of laws and rules as a good citizen, a loyal employee, and/or as a supportive neighbor *when* the observance of those laws or rules poses *no harm,* *no injustice*, or *no absurdity* to yourself – *or* to your fellowman. You must come to understand exceptions exist relative to all rules. In fact, it is the exceptions that establish (prove) the rule! This is a long-standing precept of juris-prudence (the philosophy of law)! Without acknowledging this principle, you, *should* you have OCPD, can find yourself in a **great deal** of trouble! A liberating thought is:

'I will *only* obey those laws or observe rules that are applicable to the situation, and in the best interest of all'

Now, who does one have to <u>be</u> to take upon themselves the prerogative of assessing the suitability or relevance of a law or rule? Certainly not a judge, lawyer, policeman, congressman, or senator, *alone*. No! The only authority you need as a human being is the ability to exercise your innate **discriminating intelligence**! And should you believe that a law does <u>*not*</u> apply (for the reasons stated above), you have both a moral **right** and a moral **obligation** not to observe it! Let common sense prevail! Now, go to the next page to see illustrations for the above.

Here are some examples that will help you to see how rules can be safely and wisely and for practical reasons ignored:

<u>Example 1</u>

When facing the entrance and the exit doors to a business establishment where the doors are clearly labelled as such, walk _into_ the door labelled **exit**, or walk _out_ _of_ the door labelled **entrance**. (This is done all the time at retail stores, such as Wal-Mart, which has automatic sliding (to the side into the walls) glass doors.) No one will arrest you, as many, if not most, of the patrons disregard the signs!

Example 2

You are ready to drive into a large retail parking lot from a surrounding road and notice large yellow/orange arrows painted on the concrete either pointing _into_ a given opening to the large lot, or pointing _out of_ a given opening to the large lot. You can clearly see for great distances into the lot all around you, and there are no moving vehicles close by anywhere to be seen (and perhaps few, if any, cars parked out there, as well. So, you drive _into_ the opening closest to you even though the arrow on the ground is pointing **outward** into the surrounding road. There is no danger of hitting another car, and you are now much closer to the parking spot you have decided to drive into. Again, no harm is done, even though a rule may be 'technically' broken.

Granted, these two examples are hardly monumental in nature, but not a few OCPD people have difficulty 'violating' them. To deliberately go 'against' them is a good exercise in 'desensitizing' yourself to their hold on you, and freeing your restrictive thinking.

If I am truly *__overly-conscientious__*, as so many of my friends tell me, **why** is it that I do _not_ really believe this about myself? And if I am, why is this such a bad thing?

_____No. 9_____

You do not really believe that you are overly-conscientious (relative to your morally-motivated **treatment** of others), as so many of your friends tell you, because your degree of conscientiousness, *to you*, **is** normal. In other words, because the OCPD tendency is to go to _extremes_, to _overdo_, to _overextend_, this is all you have ever known. It **feels** natural to you. But, just because something feels natural, or true, does not make it is.

For example: Because a person has felt inferior to other human beings all their life does _not_ mean that they are. All human beings are **equal** relative to their rights as a member of the human family. All people are **equally** deserving of respect and common decency. To think otherwise is to entertain a false belief, no matter how one 'feels' about it!

Now, a primary way for you to determine whether your actions are the expression of being overly-conscientious, is for you to carefully take note of the _kinds_ of feelings this overture of yours toward another generates in you. If you can ascertain and realize that you are 1) going to _greater_ lengths than most, 2) going to _unnecessary_ lengths, or 3) going to more _unusually_ demanding lengths, just to show your conscientiousness toward another, you are more than likely engaging in overly-conscientious behavior.

> **'I will do what is right, but I will not _over_-do any conscientious gesture of good will'**

In other words, this is behavior that is uncalled for, unexpected, not warranted by the circumstances, (possibly even not wanted) and most often can be detrimental to yourself and the recipient of your _over-concern for their feelings_. It is an inappropriate _over_-focus on another's feelings. But, it is the only manner of interacting with the world you know.

Over-concern is a manifestation of unwarranted anxiety and fear on your part that something bad is going to happen to yourself (or another) *if* you do not display toward them *extra*-ordinary measures of attention. It tends to feed a vicious cycle.

You are engaging in worry and apprehension you are accustomed to! Over-conscientiousness is your attempt to over-protect another's feelings, so as not to hurt them, but is inappropriate (not healthfully applicable) for adults, for if accepted, would create juvenile dependency and discourage adult self-reliance.

An over-conscientiousness towards others often speaks more to your **_own_** inner *inadequacies*, *insecurities*, and *weaknesses* than to another's supposed (though mistaken) needs for and expectations of your further assistance, contact, interactions or participation with them.

Your motivations, here, are primarily to relieve _your_ anxiety, not to actually reassure the other person, although you likely are not consciously aware of this. It is all a matter of accurate and insightful discernment. Something the OCPD person needs to become aware they are lacking in, and then seek to cultivate and develop through study (such as this volume), or guidance from a friend.

How can I **discern** the difference between the important and _un_-important, or the relevant and _ir_-relevant, or **what carries greater** or **lesser weight** in any given matter? I often have real difficulty with this!

You can discern the difference between important and _not-so_-important matters, and relevant and _not-so_-relevant matters (such as competing decisions to be made, or similar actions to be taken), etcetera, only by 1) _clear thinking,_ 2) _careful analysis,_ and 3) _studied pondering of the matter at hand._ OCPD people often are weak in these areas by nature, but seeking council of experts or people knowledgeable on the subject can be indispensable in helping you to arrive at clarity on what, to you, is a confusing subject. An encouraging thought, here, is:

'I <u>will</u> develop the capability to accurately weigh one option against another by practice, and *more* practice'

Again, it is a matter of practice in developing decision-making skills. Also, should you be an OCPD person, you will need to address your very probable fear of taking responsibility for your thinking, and of your reluctance to do so because you think you may be cognitively slow or deficient, due to health problems or sleep disturbances. But, once you realize that you are fully capable of sound and accurate discernment (provided you have no *actual* brain damage due to accident or birth defect), you can then move forward and begin to make better and *better* decisions as to what is most important and what is not.

Why is it that I feel I am open-minded (receptive to new ideas or arguments), when so many other people tell me that I am *close-minded* – and **resistant** to **different ideas**?

You feel you are open-minded, firstly, because most people realize open-mindedness is viewed as a positive and desirable trait, and you wish to be accounted as one who possesses this desirable trait. Secondly, the OCPD person believing themselves to be *always* right (or nearly always so!), of necessity then, **must** view themselves as being rightly open-minded. And, thirdly, the OCPD person genuinely feels, by nature, that they are open to new ideas or suggestions, *but* that those ideas and suggestions presented to them virtually always are poor ones, or are too counter (opposed) to their own mental stance or position to have any validity. So, to address these factors, a helpful thought, here, is:

'I will remind myself that though I may think myself open-minded, it is *possible* I may <u>not</u> be'

Of course, believing others' ideas are <u>always</u> deficient is a mental delusion because not **all** alternatives are **always** going to be worthy of dismissal or disregard. Some must have value if only by the law of averages! Therefore, it is necessary for the OCPD person to bear uppermost in mind their great **predisposition** to actually be close-minded (as evidenced by so many people telling them so), and to make every effort to remedy this situation for their own good.

How is it that what I perceive as **determination** (a positive trait) on my part, is so often viewed by others as my own **stubbornness** (a negative trait)? What distinction am I overlooking here? Who is right?

You perceive your determination (*supposed*) as a positive trait, which it is, while others view it as stubbornness, a negative trait, because more likely than not you ARE being stubborn! OCPD people have an unhealthy propensity to **be** stubborn, which means having a dogged determination *not* to change their attitude or position on a given matter, *especially in spite of good arguments or sound reasons to do so.* If you, as an OCPD person, wish to enjoy a greater ease of interaction with others, you simply must work on eliminating stubbornness in your psyche. Remember, determination refers to a person's resolve, or willpower, a firmness of purpose to do or accomplish something. It has to do with single-mindedness and strength of character. Always, it is a positive quality greatly admired and respected. An illuminating thought, here, is:

'I will be careful to *distinguish* between stubbornness and determination. One *dishonors* me, the other honors me'

Stubbornness, on the other hand, has to do with 'being difficult', unreasonable, and as one writer noted, being 'perversely unyielding'. Stubbornness speaks to being obstinate, and there is no socially redeeming value to it. Often, there is an arrogance associated with it, and a false pride.

If I **stop _accusing_** others of wrong-doing, and 'hold my tongue', will they not just continue to take advantage of me?

When you stop making it an active, ongoing practice of accusing others of wrongdoing (with perhaps a self-righteous look on your face, wide eyes, and an accusing tone), the first thing you will find is that your relationships will immediately improve. When you accuse another of violating an ethical law or moral principle, you are figuratively pointing a finger at them as guilty and worthy of blame. What many people seem to forget, here, is that they can deter or discourage another from taking advantage of them by simply telling them you do not want them to engage in that activity again. Tell them directly it is not acceptable to you. Say 'I would appreciate it very much if you will not do that again.' You do not have to make a big deal out of it, nor bring drama into it. Simply be pleasant, but firm, in conveying your position that the behavior is disturbing to you, and that you will not tolerate that action, or behavior, or kind of talk again. Recite:

'I'll refrain from *accusing* others of wrongdoing, but will *still* ask they change or cease doing an unacceptable behavior'

Remember, you often do _not_ even have to mention the word 'wrong' or 'poor behavior' or 'blame'. Just 'stick to the facts' of telling such a person to 'Please refrain from doing that when you are with me', or 'I don't want you to do that, again, please, as it hinders my ability to concentrate', or 'What you are doing interferes with my work schedule', and the like. It often works.

Is there a **Master discipline** or **Ideal practice** of *all* those listed in this book that is likely to produce the quickest results in the overcoming of my OCPD tendencies?

If there is **a Master discipline** to be utilized for your highest good, in the least amount of time, to overcome your OCPD tendencies, it is that of the practice of **Mindfulness**. This is a quality or state of mind wherein you become the 'detached observer' of your thoughts and feelings. You 'distance yourself' from them, in that you 'stand back' in your mind and view them as would an impartial observer, not judging them as right or wrong, necessarily, but noting the *content* (nature), *motivation* (reason), and *intention* (desired outcome) of those thoughts. The great value of this mental/emotional self-monitoring practice is that when you become *fully conscious* of what you are thinking, you can then **consciously decide** whether or not you really wish to give voice to it. (This way, you avoid automatic and unthinking voicing of your thoughts, which after said cannot be recalled.) A protecting thought to remember daily is:

'I will remind myself to be <u>mindful</u> of my thoughts to avoid saying *anything* not in my or another's best interest.'

You pause long enough to say, for example, 'Oh, yes, this is a critical thought' or 'Oh, yes, that is a controlling thought'. And, once you have correctly identified it, you can judge (weigh) whether it will be truly advantageous to the listener, and to yourself. You can ask the triune question of 'Is it *truly* helpful? Is it relationship-*fostering*? Is it *genuinely* wise?' **_That_** will settle it.

When I realize that I have just **said** or **done something** that is **inappropriate**, particularly due to my OCPD tendencies, how can I overcome my hesitancy (or, embarrassment) to apologize?

When you *suddenly* *realize* you have said or done something inappropriate, particularly due to your OCPD tendencies, you can overcome your hesitancy to apologize by reminding yourself we all make mistakes, occasionally, and that your admission of an error in judgment or in action is **the hallmark** of a *growing*, *learning*, *progressing* human being. Tell yourself you will become **stronger** for your admission, for you will, and others will view you as one who is just like themselves, not perfect, but in the process of becoming better. And, in future instances where you make a mistake, it will become more and *more* easier to say, 'Forgive me, I am sorry. I did not really intend to do that. My mistake.' Also, it is human nature to feel embarrassment when such occasions arise, but, again, this is an unnecessary emotion we **impose** upon ourselves, though it appears to arise spontaneously. (Our subconscious thoughts actually dictate this feeling.) A freeing affirmation to recall is:

'I will be <u>quick</u> to apologize, *where appropriate*, and called for, but I will *<u>not</u>* cling to embarrassment'

And since we are the ones who impose it, we can <u>neutralize</u> it by <u>becoming</u> <u>clear</u> in our own minds about the fact that it really does not serve us, nor another. That awkwardness, self-consciousness, or shame is our vital life energy expended to no useful purpose. It is part of the 'lower self' that would try to convince you that you deserve to be thought less of than you are.

How can I **keep** **from** thinking of myself as defective, or damaged, or a failure when I seem to so often fall short of my, and others', expectations?

_____No. 16_____

You can keep from thinking of yourself as defective, or damaged, or as a failure when you 'fall short' of your, or another's, expectations by **forcefully** reminding yourself of the following: You, irrespective of your having OCPD, the *REAL* you, the *AUTHENTIC* you, the often *HIDDEN* you, is, as an ancient wisdom text reads, **'fearfully and wonderfully made'.** Never forget that! Be continually mindful of it! This evaluation and actual **fact** cannot change, nor can it be marred by man. True, this Masterpiece of a Creation that you are, and all of your many healthy talents, may be _obscured_ by your having been mistreated, or your believing lies about yourself, or life, or by unhealthy habits you have unwittingly adopted. But, that changes nothing relative to your essential wondrous being! An empowering reminder here is:

'I will _dwell_ upon my intrinsic, Wonderful Worth, and not be misled to think otherwise'

YOU are not defective, nor damaged, nor a failure, per se. It is only a number of your acquired ways of interacting with the world that are in need of revision, *if* you are to experience the life you are meant to live and wholeheartedly desire. Change those unproductive 'ways' and <u>dramatically</u> change the quality of your life experience. And, without a doubt, you can do it!

Now that I **totally acknowledge** I have OCPD, a mental illness, what can I do to prevent myself from feeling *inferior* to others?

Now that you have totally acknowledged to yourself that you have OCPD, a mental illness, and to prevent yourself from feeling inferior to others, all you have to do is to ***also*** **acknowledge** your **fundamental equality** with all people, no matter what their station is in life, no matter how talented or gifted they are, no matter what their accomplishments may be. If you could but know, *every single individual* on this planet has what are called demerits, character defects or deficiencies, and psychological disturbances of one type or another. True, the degree may be quite _less_ than yours, or it might be considerably _greater_ than yours. No matter. All people fall somewhere within a spectrum of human characteristics. It is called a **continuum**. A wonderful phrase to remember periodically is:

'I can <u>fully</u> acknowledge my OCPD _without_ having to feel inferior, _one wit_, to anyone else'

And the bottom line is that there are always people before (or below) you on the scale, and there will always be people after (or above) you on the scale. (That is, *until*, as some believe, the 'unfoldment' of the human species reaches an apex of development, wherein **all** individuals reach the same high plateau of skill development, psychological maturity, and mental health.) And who can say, such a lofty dream as that may *yet* come true!

How long will it be before I have **gained** a **Mastery** over all of my unnatural and hurtful desires to <u>curtail</u> the rights of others?

_____No. 18_____

The time involved for you to have overcome your unnatural and hurtful desires to curtail the native-born rights of others will be the time it takes you to have **fully realized** that attempting to control others goes against the very intention and '**Prime Directive**' of the Universe (according to a multitude of wise men and women of previous ages, and of our time): That directive was popularized in a science fiction television series which began in the 1960's, as *non-interference* in the affairs of other worlds (on other planets), allowing them to unfold and develop as a civilization at their own pace; but, it also spoke to allowing *individuals* the freedom to make their own decisions, to chart their own course in life, and to adopt their own style of living, born of their own innate inclinations, personal desires, goals, and dreams. A refreshing reminder of this great gift to mankind is:

'I will, more than *anything* else, be <u>mindful</u> of the Great Law of Freedom, granting the right to all to live as *they* choose'

So it bears repeating. When you **wholly recognize** that for you to seek to curtail, restrict, or deprive others of their personal freedoms, or when you strive to control another's thoughts, choices, decisions, and actions, you are violating this Universal Law of Free Will. Such 'breaches' of conduct will _not_ serve you.

Should I **confide** in any *particular* person that I have OCPD, and if so, for what reasons? What persons should I *not* confide in?

Certainly, to confide in another person that you have OCPD can be **very much** to your *advantage*. After all, you have no reason to feel ashamed that you have this condition. Millions have it, and for all intents and purposes, it is just another situation that challenges people to grow and more fully live. But, if we are talking about truly 'opening up your *heart*' to someone, then a **truly** close friend, alone, would be best. With such a trusted confidante at your disposal, that person could serve as a valued supporter of you as you meet this condition's unique challenges day by day. This person could help you, with your invitation, to better analyze your speech and actions, help you to determine any incorrectness, or flaws, in your thinking, and serve as a cheerleader for you when you have periods of doubt, discouragement, or dismay. A helpful thought to recall is:

'I can safely confide in a *trusted* friend that I have OCPD, but there is _no_ need to divulge my business to others'

Also, it may not always be advisable to depend upon a spouse for a 'constructive critique' of any manner of your behavior you ask their input on, as there may be a *built-in bias* that would not serve the fullness of Truth. Someone removed from the immediate family situation, in most instances, probably, would be best, as they would tend to be more objective and have a kind of 'professional detachment' that is so helpful in these kinds of situations.

Should my having OCPD be a **major factor** in my choice of a profession or a livelihood? And if so, why?

Your having OCPD *most assuredly should* be considered a major factor in your choice of a profession or livelihood because certain skill sets OCPD people *naturally* possess to a high degree can be used to greatest advantage in corresponding positions requiring those skills. For example, because OCPD people are very rule conscious, detail-oriented, and reach for 'perfection', the following occupations are often ideal and offer much welcome challenge and fulfillment to them: accountant, court clerk, editor, engineer, medical transcriptionist, computer programmer, real estate agent, teacher, or even a travel agent, just to name a few. These positions, in effect, best showcase the OCPD person's true interests and talents, and not infrequently, many OCPD people are naturally drawn to them. But, if you, should you be an OCPD person, find yourself in a position where the rules are vague or incompletely defined, or where strict exactness is not required, *or even desired* by management, due to monetary or time constraints, or where you must continually interact with co-workers of varying personality types, you may well find yourself quite unhappy and dissatisfied with the work culture there. Clearly, you need to be in a position where your unique constellation of highly valued traits are appreciated and best utilized for the benefit of all. A good admonition to adopt is:

> **'I will seek out a position that utilizes to the _full_ my highly valued skills of precision, rule adherence, and excellence'**

(Refer back to <u>Occupations</u> <u>or</u> <u>Fields</u> <u>Best</u> <u>Suited</u> <u>for</u> <u>the</u> <u>OCPD</u> <u>Person</u> narrative section and corresponding table in **OCPD's Only Hope** volume)

Should I *mention* to a **<u>first</u> date** of mine, in whom I have a genuine **romantic interest**, that I have OCPD?

<hr>

No. 21

To mention on a *first* date that you have OCPD is likely to invite many questions from your partner about your condition, since OCPD is still relatively unknown, and set the tone (if not the primary topic of conversation) for the *entire* luncheon, dinner, and outing engagement. And should that happen, you might find yourself attempting to 'explain, justify, and defend' yourself in a sheepish, somewhat less-than-positive, embar-rassed way. That being the case, there really is no good reason to broach the topic at that time. A first date is meant to be a lighthearted and enjoyable sharing of some basic, non-controversial personal information in this early, acquaintance establishing, getting-to-know-you-better, come-together. Keep it that way by being as natural and relaxed as you can. Remind yourself of this:

> 'I have _no need_ to mention to a first date I have OCPD, as another more _appropriate_ time will arise'

And do _not_ fall into the trap of feeling you are being judged. Should you make a mistake in speech or table manners, or the like, acknowledge it to yourself and then _let it go_ as we all make mistakes, and the well-adjusted, comfortable-with-himself (or herself), mature, caring person readily accepts this of themselves, _as they will of you_. Because of all this, you can truly relax. Later on, after the two of you have become better acquainted, an appropriate time will present itself and become clear to you that 'then and there' a sharing of your condition can take place.

Will I ever become **completely free** from _all_ of my OCPD obsessions and compulsions, and _all_ their associated symptoms?

One day, dear friend, you _will_ become free of all of your OCPD obsessions and compulsions (or at the very least, be able to control and manage those strong tendencies) and symptoms, _if_, and this little word actually is a very big word, _if_, you are **determined** to do so. There is virtually nothing in life that will not yield to a determined and consciously exercised will, coupled with a powerful desire to attain a given end. If, in the OCPD constellation of traits that beleaguer you and torment others, you hold onto _only one_ – let that one trait be an

'Obsessional Desire' to be free of OCPD! Yet, this will not be a *desire that makes you feel driven or frantic in a wild and uncontrolled way*, but rather an ongoing healthful desire, a forward-looking desire, to attain freedom through **perseverance** of action and will. It means making up your mind once and for all to become free! Ralph Waldo Emerson, that celebrated sage of New England in the mid-1800's wrote, 'Once you make a decision, *the universe conspires to make it happen.*' Let this Truth comfort you as you continue day by day to achieve your goal. All of your efforts will be worth it. Tell yourself often:

> 'I recognize the fact I _can_ become free of my OCPD traits, for others have done so, and so can I'

With your commitment to the self-discipline of continual **mindfulness**, which involves analysis of your thought, and _if you want it badly enough_, you _will_ succeed! You _will_ become free!

Are there _any_ circumstances under which I should definitely keep my OCPD condition and habits a **secret**?

_____No. 23_____

The circumstances under which you should definitely keep your OCPD condition and habits a secret would be those circumstances where you **feel reasonably certain** your revealing it might, 1) cause another to become _uneasy_ around you, or 2) cause another to inquire about your condition to an uncalled-for degree (possibly causing _you_ to feel uneasy), or 3) cause another to _discriminate_ against you due to their ignorance or stupidity. Now, the Truth is, unless you have acquired at least a _degree_ of **Insight**, already, it will be nearly

impossible for another _not_ to become aware that your behaviors are out of the ordinary, annoying, troublesome, or problematic. But, the good news is that _if_ you are able to ask this question of yourself, and reflect upon it in a detached, objective way, then that would strongly indicate (if not prove) that should you have OCPD, you most assuredly, and thankfully, possess **Insight** into its 'workings' and 'manifestations'. A helpful thought to rehearse is:

'I will evaluate each person as to whether it is wise to intentionally and verbally disclose my OCPD condition'

The condition (or manifestations), itself, can hardly be kept a secret by those people who have no **Insight**, but presuming that you have acquired a healthful measure (having read thus far), you are in the process of consciously curtailing the number of occurrences, and lessening their degree of severity. Don't just tell everyone, tell few, as you are _recovering_ – and being healed.

Will it be **necessary** for me, as an OCPD person, to continue any particular disciplines (as outlined in your book) *for the rest of my life*, to ensure I don't fall back into my old self-defeating ways?

_____No. 24_____

It will be necessary for you, as an OCPD person, to continue the disciplines for the rest of your life to ensure you don't fall back into your old self-defeating ways for the **same reason** that any other (_non_-OCPD) person would be well-advised to do so. And that same reason is that the disciplines presented, herein, correspond to **universal principles** of **harmonious human conduct** which unfailingly work when understood, practiced consistently, and correctly applied. So, the question really becomes who would _not_ want to practice these disciplines and to 'embody' these principles for a lifetime to create a joyous life of friendly cooperation and sweet rapport? Why, no one, *of course!* (That is, except for the OCPD person whose beliefs are so intractable and entrenched that they are totally *incapable* of altering them, being 'blind' to the self-evident (to everyone else) Truth before her or him.) A powerful phrase to recall on occasion is:

'I am _more than_ willing to discipline my mind and heart for a lifetime, as the rewards are assured and immense'

You will, of course, in time, not have to *necessarily* refer back to this book (or reminder cards, or meditations, or tables, etc.) to be reminded of these Truths, for at some point, you will have <u>internalized</u> them sufficiently to have them arise in your consciousness naturally and automatically. No longer, thereafter, will it be 'work' even to the least degree. You will have arrived.

If *some* of your techniques to prevent or lessen certain OCPD behaviors <u>not</u> work for me, does this mean I am utilizing them **incorrectly**?

_____No. 25_____

Should some of the techniques (mental models) to prevent or lessen certain OCPD behaviors *not* work for you, this most likely means you are as yet unskilled in their practice. Like any other new activity to which you are unaccustomed, there is a 'learning curve' involved. You will, in all likelihood, falter and 'fail' from time to time in use of these techniques, but this does not mean you are performing the practice in a wrong fashion. It simply means you need more time to grow comfortable with *refraining* from saying or doing something, or more proficient in executing the chosen technique at hand. Here is an encouraging statement to bolster your confidence at times such as these:

'I will *not* be discouraged should a given technique to 'rein in' my OCPD traits not work for a while. It will, in time'

For example, you find yourself, unexpectedly, beginning to heatedly argue a point of debate with a relative, or co-worker, out of *force of habit*. As soon as you realize this, you begin to remind myself of the futility of arguing, and of all the damage it can do. You attempt to quiet your mind, and regain your composure, lest the argument escalate into an angry 'row'. But, to your dismayed surprise, you just continue on 'countering' your, now-viewed, opponent's rebuttals. Don't despair. In time, with further practice, you _will_ gain mastery over your emotions, and 'tame' your OCPD. Your present 'need' to argue is the real culprit.

Should I attempt to practice **all** of the mental disciplines *at* *the* *same* *time*, or should I **focus**, primarily, on only one or two?

_____No. 26_____

Practicing all of the disciplines at the same time, or focusing on, primarily, one or two, will take place mostly of its own accord. That is to say, one some days, you will find yourself, of *necessity*, having to focus on one or two, as the *particular* concerns (criticizing, judging, attempting to control, etc.) will call for special focus or immediate attention as they arise, or just *before* they arise. While the other disciplines (mental constructs, or mental models of viewing your 'inner landscape', your interior urges, and the outer situation) will then naturally, but only temporarily, fade into the background. An excellent memory aid here would be:

'I will place my attention upon _whichever_ OCPD trait is <u>attempting</u> to arise, and deal with it _before_ it arises'

Further, what will be transpiring as you practice the various mental disciplines designed to deal with _different_ OCPD traits, is that, again, in time, your newly-learned responses will take place automatically, reflecting the appropriate discipline on your part. Also, the human mind _can_ only focus (fully) on one matter at a time as the stream of consciousness is linear at the conscious level. So, precisely speaking, the undesired OCPD traits that arise can only be dealt with in a sequential manner, or in a 'one-after-the-other' fashion. Though still true, when practicing the **'Acquiring Insight Exercises'**, you will be giving more attention to one pre-selected OCPD idea as you are able, and as time and circumstance permit.

When is the **best time** of the day to read this book, and within what environment, to afford me the **greatest benefit**?

_____No. 27_____

The best time of day to read this book, and the best environment, to afford you the greatest benefit is that time of day when you are the _most_ relaxed and _least_ accessible to outside disturbances. These two factors perhaps more so than any others, whether they be morning, mid-day, evening, or at night for that matter, have been shown to be the most conducive to learning new material and retaining it for future recall. Now, if those two main factors coincide with your being a morning person or a night person, and so on, then you have doubly insured the optimal circumstances for study. And, of course, the final component would be the location. For some, it would be by the ocean, for another upon a mountain top, and yet another still, near a prairie where deer and antelope play. The following affirmation relates directly to these factors:

'I will seek out the optimal study time and environment which corresponds to my own personal tastes and needs'

If you have not tried reading in the middle of the night, by the way, when other household members have long since retired, and the out of doors is wholly quiet and serene, you might wish to do it some time. Numerous people have found such a time to be as if one were in a different world entirely. A world where you may be able to achieve a *greater* *clarity* and a *deeper* *understanding* of all you read and ponder. **Insight** has been known to 'flash' into consciousness at such times. Perhaps so with you.

<u>Acquiring Insight Affirmations</u>

(At a glance)

No. 1

Today, I choose to criticize no one

No. 2

Today, I choose not to complain about anything

No. 3

Today, I will make no attempt to control others

No. 4

Today, I will worry about nothing or no one

No. 5

Today, I will not be a slave to perfectionism

No. 6

Today, I will not allow non-applicable rules to govern my life

No. 7

Today, I will be conscientious, but not overly so

No. 8

Today, I will discern wisely, keeping the big picture in view

No. 9

Today, I will be agreeably flexible in thought and deed

No. 10

Today, I will judge no one nor anything

No. 11

Today, I will speak ill of no one or no thing

A Solemn Pledge

To *My Self* to Uncover my <u>True</u> Self

I pledge to <u>*seek*</u> the Truth about my Life even if it is uncomfortable

I pledge to regularly <u>*examine*</u> my thoughts for errors in logic

I pledge to routinely <u>*monitor*</u> my thinking to be aware of my mood

I pledge to carefully <u>*analyze*</u> my motives for improper ones

I pledge to <u>*pause*</u> before I speak to ensure my speech is beneficial

I pledge to *practice* self-discipline in curbing any impulse to criticize

I pledge to *demonstrate* self-restraint to prevent me from complaining

I pledge to *be wary* of my controlling nature and to halt it

I pledge to *oust* worry from my consciousness before it envelops me

I pledge to *question* every tendency to 'perfection' and to curtail it

I pledge to *exercise* greater flexibility for all the right reasons

I pledge to *disregard* rules that disregard me and those I love

I pledge to *judge* no man, as I would have no man judge me

I pledge to *accept* the perfection of seeming 'imperfection'

I pledge to *adopt* a positive attitude in all my conversations

I pledge to *maintain* order, but not permit it to 'order' (dictate to) me

I pledge to keep this promise to myself for as long as I shall live!

My Daily Commitment

To *My Self* to Conquer OCPD

Today, I Reaffirm my Overall Commitment:

To **become free** of all OCPD traits that <u>harm</u> my life

To **break free** of all OCPD tendencies that <u>hurt</u> my relationships

To **be liberated** from all OCPD inclinations that <u>diminish</u> my person

To **find deliverance** from all OCPD obsessions that <u>fatigue</u> my mind

To **obtain release** from all OCPD compulsions that <u>exhaust</u> my body

To **claim liberty** from all OCPD urges
that <u>imprison</u> my soul

To **escape from** all OCPD promptings
that <u>shrivel</u> my spirit, *And*

To **submit no longer** to all OCPD
influences that <u>*blind*</u> me

to all the wonder, beauty, joy, majesty,
mystery,

and natural perfection of life,

wherein I can allow others to be **who**
they are,

without any need on my part to change
them, or desire to re-arrange them

KNOWING

Such commitment will <u>*assure*</u> me

Of a Brighter Tomorrow!

Positive Outlook Declarations

I have been given the *Stupendous* Gift of Life! Today!

(I dare *not* take it for granted)

I am a *Miraculous* Being filled with **Tremendous Purpose**! Today!

(My life is not an accident)

I possess *Powers* and *Abilities* yet unknown to Myself! Today!

(And I thrill to the thought of discovering them)

I am a *very Valuable* **Person** Who would be difficult to replace! Today

(No, make that – *impossible* to replace)

My every moment is filled with **Promise**, **Opportunity**,

And great **Importance!** Today!

(If, I only have the wisdom to see it)

I will <u>not</u> think less of **Myself** than I should! Today!

(I choose to be known for who I really am, <u>*no*</u> more and <u>*no*</u> less)

I can **Enjoy** this day if I <u>*determine*</u> to do so! Today!

(It is all a matter of setting my intention)

I will remain **Open** and **Receptive** to all the **wonders** about me! Today!

(And be expectant about their appearance)

I am **bigger** than <u>any</u> of my circumstances! Today!

(*<u>Nothing</u>* can conquer my indomitable spirit)

Thus it has been recited! Today!

(*So it <u>IS</u> and <u>SHALL</u> be so*)

Farewell Message

Dear friend,

Congratulations! You have now completed your survey of twenty-five of the most **basic**, yet _critical_, questions concerning OCPD, and their highly practical answers. This fundamental education will stand you in good stead as you incorporate these solutions into your daily life.

It is my sincere hope that you will, now, if not already having done so, obtain my flagship volume, **OCPD's Only Hope of Psychological Wellness**, from which these vital questions and answers were derived. And having done the above, you have journeyed *far* in your undertaking to complete the full course of instruction and make it an active part of your life. You will rightfully be very proud that you have done so. You will have reached deep into your inner being, courageously challenging the validity or falsity of *long-held* assumptions, opinions, beliefs, and attitudes, as difficult as that was, or will be, at times, and searched your soul to arrive at the Truth of the 'whys' and 'wherefores' of your life. And though you will feel, perhaps, embarrassed on occasion in doing so, you will have 'stayed the course' and confronted your deepest insecurities, false pride, arrogance, adult regressive tendencies (childishness), inaccurate thinking, and even outright ignorance in some cases. But, no matter, for as that early 20th century American sage, Will Rogers, once said, 'We are **all** ignorant, but not about the same things.'

However, as regards Obsessive Compulsive Personality Disorder, that will no longer be said of you to your great credit. For after your having read this book, and its source volume, studiously, and with an open mind, you will now know far more about this subject than *ninety-nine* percent of all other people. And, more importantly, you will possess the intellectual and psychological tools required to successfully confront this formidable disorder (*if*, indeed, you did find it within your nature) *head-on* whenever it should seek to manifest *through* you in a weak, forgetful, or distracted moment of your life.

The source volume begins with a hearty 'Congratulations' to you for 'your *willingness* and *open-mindedness* to explore, reflect upon, and consider the validity of the vital message of this book, and its possible direct application to you.' Let this pocket book, now, come to a close with an equally-sincere, even more hearty: '**Congratulations!**' You will have, without a doubt, earned it as you make steady progress toward extinguishing every remnant of harmful OCPD traits from your life!

And, from this point on, whether you have OCPD, or *not*, refer back to this book periodically as an advocate for **clear**, **accurate**, **mature**, wholly **sane thinking**. Thinking that upholds the principles of personal liberty, autonomy, self-determination, and the freedom to decide one's own way, even in the seemingly 'little things' of everyday household and workplace life. For by extending these 'inalienable rights' to all others, you, my now-wiser friend, will ensure those same rights – for yourself.

Godspeed!

Mack W. Ethridge
President, NFHR, Inc.

I Believe in Myself
Affirmations

Fundamentals

I Believe I AM a person of worth and dignity because I am human

I Believe I AM deserving of courtesy and respect by virtue of being born

I Believe I AM a valuable member of the human race

I Believe I AM a unique creation, unlike any other person on earth

I Believe I AM a complete person, whether I have a mate, or not

I Believe I AM bigger than my circumstances

I Believe I AM a Victor over any situation as long as I continue to try

I Believe my life is purposeful and meaningful and worthwhile

I Believe no one can diminish me without my permission

OCPD Related Basics

I Believe criticism is rarely an optimal solution

I Believe complaining seldom does anyone any good

I Believe controlling another person shrivels my soul

I Believe worrying is negative faith and feeds despair

I Believe perfection encompasses the seemingly 'imperfect'

I Believe 'everything in its place' should pertain more to my inner world, than to my outer world

I Believe judging another is an automatic judgment upon myself

I Believe being positive lifts up the entirety of the world

I Believe being flexible is a sign of great maturity

I Believe rules and laws or policies must serve man or they are invalid

I Believe I AM only responsible for myself and my pre-adult children

I Believe I can make a mistake and become wiser thereby

I Believe I can be at peace though others are irresponsible or careless

25 <u>KEY</u> QUESTIONS

The OCPD Person <u>MUST</u> Ask!

(And <u>*Have*</u> Answered!)

Finis

Excerpted from

OCPD's <u>*Only*</u> Hope of Psychological Wellness!

(Textbook Volume)